I Am Harriet Tubman

By Grace Norwich

Illustrated by
Ute Simon

SCHOLASTIC INC.

ISBN 978-0-545-48436-7

10 9 8 7 6 5 4 3 2 1   13 14 15 16 17 18/0

Printed in the U.S.A.   40
First printing, January 2013

Cover illustration by Mark Fredrickson
Interior illustrations by Ute Simon

Contents

Introduction

I was born a slave *and* a woman. In my time, you couldn't get much lower than that. And even as I grew up, I never reached much taller than five feet. So I was a slave, a woman, *and* small. Not exactly hero material.

No one who looked at me could have imagined that I would do what I ended up doing in my lifetime. After I escaped from slavery on the Underground Railroad, I returned to the South again and again and again, to make more trips and rescue more slaves. People call me brave, but I was also just stubborn. I hated slavery so much that I couldn't stand to see any of my family, friends, or even strangers forced to be a victim of it.

That would have been enough to prove there was more to me than met the eye. But that's not all I did. During the Civil War, I was a spy and

nurse—and even helped lead a battle! After the war, I continued to help people in need.

Long after slavery ended, I was still busy fighting for the rights of women who couldn't vote, poor veterans who didn't have a place to live, and old folks who needed someone to care for them.

> "I had reasoned this out in my mind. There was one of two things I had a *right* to, liberty or death; if I could not have one, I would have the other; for no man should take me alive; I should fight for my liberty as long as my strength lasted."

Though I was born with what some may have called disadvantages, I led a life anyone would be proud of. I may have been small, but I sure put up a big fight. I am Harriet Tubman.

People You Will Meet

HARRIET TUBMAN:
A small woman, barely five feet tall, who became a giant of the Underground Railroad, making nineteen trips south to bring slaves to freedom.

HARRIET "RIT" GREEN*:
Harriet's mother, who was born into slavery in Maryland after her own mother, a member of the Ashanti tribe, was taken from Africa.

BEN ROSS*:
Harriet's father, who was a lumberman (which was a rare job for a slave).

JOHN TUBMAN*:
A free man who married
Harriet, but refused
to go north to escape
slavery and eventually
remarried.

WILLIAM H. SEWARD:
A senator from Auburn,
New York, and an outspoken
abolitionist, who later
became President Lincoln's
secretary of state. He
supported Harriet's work, and
sold her a piece of land in his
hometown at a good price.

ABRAHAM LINCOLN:
The sixteenth president of
the United States, elected
in 1860, whose stance on
slavery caused several
states to leave the Union.

NELSON DAVIS:
A Civil War veteran and
former slave who married
Harriet when she was in
her forties.

* Artist's rendering

Time Line

about 1821

Araminta Ross, who would later be known as Harriet Tubman, is born on a plantation in Maryland to Harriet and Ben Ross.

about 1834

Harriet defies orders to help tie up another slave and gets hit with a weight by an overseer, causing her a life of headaches and narcolepsy.

December 1850

Harriet travels back to Maryland to bring her niece Kessiah to freedom.

Christmas 1854

After several tries at escaping, Harriet's brothers are finally successful in fleeing to Canada with the help of their sister.

1862

Harriet travels to South Carolina to work on the side of the Union army in the Civil War.

June 1863

Harriet helps lead three hundred troops in the successful Combahee River raid in South Carolina during the Civil War.

1844

Harriet marries a free black man, John Tubman.

1849

Harriet runs away and makes it to freedom in Philadelphia.

June 1857

Harriet makes the trip from her hometown to Canada with her elderly parents.

about 1859

The prominent abolitionist and senator from New York William H. Seward sells Harriet a home near Auburn, New York.

Spring 1896

Harriet buys the property near her home to create a home for the elderly.

March 10, 1913

Harriet dies of pneumonia.

Strong from the Start

Harriet Tubman didn't know what day she was born. There were no cakes or parties and there wasn't much to celebrate for a child who was expected to begin working by the time she turned five. In fact, she may not have known her birthday because most slaves didn't know how to read or write. (If a slave was caught learning how to read and write, he could have his fingers or toes cut off!)

A Baby Is Born

Recently, historians uncovered a record from March 15, 1822, of a two–dollar payment from the owner of Harriet's mother to a midwife for delivering a baby that scholars believe to be the young Harriet. So that date is now widely considered her birthday.

She might not have known the date, but from a very early age, Harriet, whose name was originally Araminta Ross, knew exactly where she came from and what she was: a slave.

As the fifth of at least nine children born to Harriet "Rit" Green and Ben Ross, Harriet was a third-generation slave on her mother's side. Her maternal grandmother, Modesty, was from Africa and was most likely a member of the Ashanti tribe. The Ashanti, known for their strength of body and spirit, greatly respected women, who were often leaders in the tribe. (Harriet, who became a historical groundbreaker, definitely inherited the leadership gene.)

In 1810, there were over one million slaves in America. Most of them were Africans from tribes that had been conquered by other tribes in Africa. Traded to European sea captains for guns, ammunition, and other goods, the slaves

Before she changed her name, everyone called Harriet "Minty" for short. Historians disagree as to when she changed her name. Some believe it was after she married. Others think she changed it after escaping slavery, which was a common practice.

were brought to America. People were stolen from their homes and treated no better than animals. The ships could carry as many as six hundred African men, women, and children. They were forced to lie side by side in the

airless hull for the long, rocky journey because there was no room to stand or sit up. Once they arrived in America, the captains exchanged them again for things that weren't available in Europe, like tobacco, rice, and cotton.

Rit, Ben, and their children all lived and worked on the Brodess **plantation** in Bucktown, Maryland. (A plantation is a large farm where crops are tended to by people who live on the estate.) Not long after Harriet was born, her father was separated from the rest of his family. Ben Ross was a skilled foreman who managed the lumber operations in the plantation's big forests. This was a rare job for a slave, so he couldn't leave when the son of the plantation's owner married, moved into his own home, and took Harriet's mother and all her children with him.

In general, slave families could be split apart at a moment's notice. Children were ripped from their parents. Husbands and wives were divided forever. Nothing was off-limits. At slave auctions all over the country, relatives were left devastated simply because owners decided it was time to sell one of their slaves.

The fact that Ben didn't get to live with his family was hard. Compared to what other

slave families had to **endure**, however, the Ross family couldn't complain. But a year or two after Rit and her children went to a new master, their worst fears came true. One of Harriet's sisters, Mariah, was sold to a slave trader in Mississippi. Deeper into the South, where Mariah was headed, conditions for slaves were even harsher than they were in Maryland. The family would never see or hear from her again.

The fear and sadness over the very real possibility of losing a loved one at any time was only a small part of the many horrors slaves faced every day. Life for a slave was backbreaking labor—without a break. They worked six days a week from the moment the sun came up until it finally set. Some slaves worked in the houses of their masters, while others worked in the fields growing and harvesting crops. Wherever their jobs were located, they were often beaten if their masters decided they weren't working hard enough.

It didn't matter if someone was sick or still just a child; everyone had to work, and work hard. By five or six years old, children were considered old enough to have jobs. Often, they started out as babysitters for the children of slave owners, or they were given tasks that, though they didn't take a lot of strength, carried heavy responsibility. By twelve, a few children were taught skills like cooking, sewing, or weaving, but most began working in the fields.

There were few comforts to console them during this endless labor. Masters fed their slaves as little as possible, because food cost money. Children usually didn't have real clothes. Instead, they wore rough, itchy sacks with holes cut out for their heads and arms.

Harriet was put in charge of taking care of her younger brothers and sisters when she was only four years old. Not surprisingly, she had some pretty funny ideas of what that meant, including a game she called "pig in a bag," where she would swing her brother around upside down by the bottom of his nightshirt. When it was late and her mother still hadn't come home, Harriet had to figure out what to feed her crying siblings. Once, after she had fed them pork, Rit returned and saw a piece

of pork hanging out of the mouth of Harriet's sleeping baby brother. She thought he had died!

At about eight years old, Harriet was hired out to a weaver's family. The weaver's home was only about 10 miles from the plantation, but it may as well have been a million. In a new place, surrounded by strangers, she cried every night on the kitchen floor, where she slept in front of the fire. The people she worked for didn't care if she was homesick or any other kind of sick. When Harriet came down with measles and spiked a fever, she was still expected to complete her daily tasks, including heading through soggy wetlands to check muskrat traps.

That was only the first of many jobs for Harriet. A couple of years later, Harriet was sent to work as a house servant. The only problem was that no one had ever taught her how to sweep or dust—and her new mistress loved her whip so much that she slept with it under her pillow. One day, Harriet was whipped five times before breakfast by her mistress, who kept finding traces of dust and dirt.

Her mistress's cruelty didn't stop Harriet from stealing a lump of sugar, which she had never tasted before. Unfortunately, the mean woman caught her and immediately went for the whip. Afraid of another beating, Harriet made a beeline for the door and didn't stop once she had run through it. She kept running and

running, although she had no idea where she
was going. In the end, she didn't have anywhere
to go and hid in the pigpen. There she remained

for five long days, fighting the pigs for scraps from the trough. By day five she was starving and had no choice but to come out.

Harriet was sure a beating from her mistress awaited her, but instead the master of the house did the beating. He struck her so hard he broke her ribs and gave her scars for life.

That wasn't the worst blow Harriet was to receive.

After Harriet had begun working for another master, she was on a shopping trip with the cook to buy supplies for the house when they ran into another slave, who was in town without permission. Soon the overseer—the person in charge of supervising slaves on the plantation—arrived, looking for the other slave. When he found him in a store, the overseer asked Harriet to help tie the slave down so he could beat him.

Harriet said no.

She didn't think about it before she said it. She simply spoke from the heart, and her heart said no.

While the overseer stood there in shock, the other slave got out of his grasp and ran for the exit. As the slave was making his getaway, the overseer grabbed a weight used for measuring and threw it toward the door. It hit Harriet in the forehead and knocked her to the ground. She was dragged, bleeding, back to the plantation. For the next couple of days, she went in and out of consciousness and came close to death. As soon as it was clear she wasn't going to die, she was sent back out to the fields with "the blood and sweat rolling down [her] face till [she] couldn't see."

When Harriet refused to take part in violence against another human being that day in the store, she proved something that would be true throughout her life; her conscience was

always stronger than any concern for her own
well-being.

A Lifelong Hurt

Harriet survived the terrible blow to her head, but for the rest of her life she suffered from awful headaches. At times, she fell asleep without warning, a condition that's called **narcolepsy**. The sleepiness could come over her while she was talking, eating, or even out in the fields. It was such a deep slumber that when an overseer hit her with a whip to wake her up, she continued to snooze. Historians now think she suffered from something called temporal lobe epilepsy from her head injury as a girl.

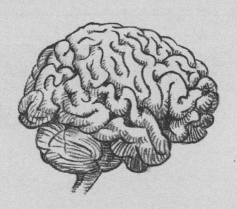

CHAPTER TWO

Runaway!

Slaves had to be extremely strong both inside and out to endure the hardship and terrible treatment they faced every day. But Harriet's strength was legendary—you can't go back to hard labor in the fields two days after a major head injury and survive if you're a weakling.

As a young woman, Harriet was still a tiny person. She stood only five feet tall, but her height and slight frame were misleading. Harriet was just as strong as most men. She

could move heavy barrels filled with goods with the best of them. People, marveling at her muscle, got a kick out of watching her work. She plowed fields and drove oxen, chopped wood and hauled logs. Her father took special pride in his daughter's remarkable ability. Ben, who had a lifetime of experience working in the forest, handed down his knowledge to his daughter (something that would come in very handy not too far in the future).

When she was about twenty-two, Harriet fell in love and married John Tubman, a free black man. But marrying a free man did not mean Harriet became free, too. Instead, she remained a slave, who could be sold and separated from her husband at any time. In fact, when a slave wanted to get married—whether to another

slave or to a free person—the slave had to ask permission from their master. If Harriet and John had children, the children also would be slaves. What a way to start a life together!

In 1849, Harriet's longtime master died, and his widow decided she would sell some

Free At Last

In 1830, about 53,000 black people living in Maryland, or one—third of all blacks living in Maryland, were free. Some bought their freedom, which was very expensive and hard to do. Others inherited their freedom after their masters died. Some free black people were descendants of Africans who came to America on their own as explorers, traders, or sailors.

of the plantation's slaves to pay off debts her husband had left. One of the slaves she wanted to put on the auction block was Harriet's niece Kessiah, who was married with children! Harriet thought about her own future. Who was headed to the auction next? She lived in fear of being separated from her family and her new husband. "[E]very time I saw a white man I was afraid of being carried away," she said.

In Harriet's mind, there were only two options: be taken away to an unknown place she didn't want to go, or run away to a place she did. She discussed her desire to flee north with John. Although he could leave Maryland anytime he wanted because he was a free man, he told Harriet under no circumstances would

he leave. She did her best to talk him into it, but he wouldn't budge. Maybe John was afraid of getting caught with Harriet, a fugitive, and being beaten or thrown in jail. Running away was the most dangerous thing a slave could do, and it was equally risky for anyone who helped that slave.

She loved her husband but could be ripped away from him at any moment. If she were sold, it would certainly be to a plantation deeper in the South, where the weather was hotter, the work harder, and the chance of ever making it north impossibly small. So Harriet made a decision that must have been very painful. She made a plan for her escape—and kept it secret from her husband.

In the middle of the night on September 17, 1849, Harriet and her brothers Ben and Henry snuck out of their cabins and headed into the darkness of a completely unknown future.

Unfortunately, it wasn't one that included freedom—at least not on this trip. Not long into their escape, Harriet and her brothers started fighting about directions. They couldn't take roads up north, so they had to stick to forests, swamps, and fields at night, when the chance of being seen was slim. Getting lost was easy— and incredibly dangerous.

Ben and Henry decided they didn't want to go on. Harriet was furious. How could they go back when they knew that the worst beating of their lives awaited them? As soon as their owner figured out they were missing, she posted a notice with a reward of $100 each if they were captured out of state, and $50 in state. When they waltzed back onto the plantation, she'd surely kill them. In the end, though, the brothers won, and despite Harriet's angry protests, they all turned back.

Harriet, however, was not one to give up,

and it wasn't long before she ran away again.
This time, she didn't take any chances. Harriet
set off for freedom alone. The dark woods and
all their strange noises weren't going to keep

her from liberty. She looked up to the North Star, the brightest in the sky, which would be her guide to Pennsylvania, and started out on the Underground Railroad.

This railroad didn't have tracks or trains. The Underground Railroad was a supersecret network of people who helped slaves trying to escape to freedom. The name came from

an incident with an escaped slave named Tice Davids. While running away from Kentucky, he swam across  the Ohio River. His master, chasing him, was mystified that Tice seemed to disappear when he got to the other side. He said Tice had found

some sort of "an underground railroad." The real Underground Railroad was comprised of thousands of white and black people, known as "conductors," who were against slavery. They provided the "stations," safe places for runaway slaves to hide. These could be attics, or hidden crawl spaces under floors, or behind shelves. Each conductor would offer the name of the next conductor. The runaways, known as

"packages," traveled at night, usually by foot but sometimes by wagon or boat. Every step on the routes that crisscrossed the country from the Mexican border to Canada was scary, because slave hunters were constantly on the lookout for escaped slaves. Conductors also faced severe consequences if they were caught helping fugitives. White people could be given big fines or be put in jail. But for blacks, the punishment could be much, much worse: They could be put to death. The people who made up the Railroad, which carried thousands to freedom, were incredibly brave. Those conductors put aside their personal safety to follow their consciences. Harriet had found her people.

The first person Harriet stayed with on her journey was a white woman who lived not too far from the plantation. A white woman! Harriet must have been startled when the door opened to reveal a white face on the other side. White people had only hurt her. Why would

this woman help her? But Harriet put her faith and life in the hands of this complete stranger, and walked through the door.

The following night, the woman gave Harriet the name of her next conductor, and the small **fugitive** was on her way. She traveled by night through swamps and forests, surviving on scraps of food or plants she knew were edible. The fear of running into a slave hunter or one of their vicious dogs fueled Harriet through her hunger and exhaustion. She never knew what was coming next. On one leg of her journey, she hid in a wagon under goods while it drove her to the next station. Mostly, though, she was alone, looking up at her big, bright North Star and moving forward.

Secret Codes

It was hard for slaves to pass along secret information to one another. Often under the watchful eye of an overseer, they had little privacy. For the most part, they didn't know how to read or write, so passing notes was impossible. How did slaves plan to escape—or pass along warnings—without being found out? Here are a few ways they created secret codes:

• **QUILTS**: These blankets, which would hang from windows without drawing attention, carried codes that gave encouragement and warnings to fugitives through their patterns.

For example, a zigzagged pattern called the Drunkard's Path was a reminder not to travel in a straight line, so that hunters would get confused.

• **SONGS**: Working in the same way as the quilts, songs had hidden meanings. "Follow the Drinking Gourd" was a song that referred to the Big Dipper, which is used to find the North Star—the main guide for slaves trying to go north.

About a hundred miles after she began,
Harriet finally crossed into Pennsylvania, a
free state. "I felt like I was in Heaven," she said
about her first taste of freedom. Harriet kept
going until she found herself in Philadelphia.

Philadelphia: Let Freedom Ring

Philadelphia at that time was the fourth–largest city in the world and had twenty thousand African Americans, who were, for the most part, free residents.

Life in Philadelphia couldn't have been more different than life on the plantation. First of all, Harriet could go where she wanted

without asking for anyone's permission. When she wasn't working as a maid or a cook, she liked to visit local parks or black-owned shops. It was amazing to live in a place where African Americans had their own businesses, went to schools, and attended their own churches.

Philadelphia was remarkable, but Harriet missed her family. Freedom wasn't as sweet when she knew they were still enslaved back home. While Harriet worked hard and diligently saved her money, she vowed to rescue her family. She didn't know how she'd do it, but when Harriet got something into her mind there was no getting it out.

In December 1850, Harriet learned that her niece Kessiah was again up for sale. (Her owner hadn't been able to sell her before.) While Harriet had everything to lose—her freedom and her life—she had no other choice than to help a member of her family who was in trouble. Returning south to Baltimore, she met up with Kessiah's husband, John Bowley,

a free man, and the two cooked up a risky and daring plan.

What they pulled off could have been a scene out of an action movie. At the auction in Cambridge, Maryland, where Kessiah and her children were being sold, John bid and bid for them until everyone else stopped and he won the auction. He didn't have the hundreds of dollars that he was supposed to hand over for his new purchase, but he didn't plan on sticking around long enough to pay up.

When the auctioneer took a break to eat, John used the confusion of the crowded auction to steal his family, who hid out in the home of a nearby white woman. That night, they took a small sailboat on a rough and treacherous two-day journey to Baltimore, where they were reunited with Harriet. That was just the start of the trip! From there, Aunt Harriet guided them from station to station on her beloved

Underground Railroad until they made it to Philadelphia.

The reward of witnessing other people experience the same joy she did upon gaining her freedom made Harriet realize her true calling: rescuing others. From that one journey with Kessiah and her family, Harriet was hooked.

In the spring of 1851, Harriet was riding the Railroad again to guide her brother Moses and two other men on her second successful trip.

Confident of her abilities to **maneuver** in enemy territory, Harriet decided to return that fall to the area of Dorchester County, where she had been a slave. Though she now had a new life, she still missed one thing from her old life—her husband, John. It was super risky, even for Harriet, but she wanted to bring her husband back with her to Philadelphia. She had worked hard to save up money for a new suit for John, which she carried with care. She knocked on his door, suit in hand, ready to reunite with her lost love. When he opened the door she discovered that John had remarried! Not only was he married to a free woman, but he made it clear he had no plans to leave her for Harriet.

Harriet was heartbroken and mad. She'd walked at least 100 miles to retrieve her husband, who no longer loved her. Well, she wasn't going to waste the 100-mile journey. Harriet channeled her anger and sadness into motivation to lead a group of four or five fugitives to freedom. Maybe she still had some emotions to work out, because she returned

not too long after to rescue as many as eleven
more. That was just the beginning.

CHAPTER THREE

A Woman on a Mission

Harriet turned into a nonstop freedom freight train.

The incredible strength and staying power she showed as a young woman working with her dad in the lumberyard made her an unbeatable conductor on the Underground Railroad. (She also took side jobs chopping wood to fund her missions.) Starting in 1852, Harriet began making at least one trip a year, but often more. By the winter of 1853–54, she made at least five trips, guiding thirty slaves safely north!

Harriet traveled up and down the East Coast so many times that she must have known the terrain like the back of her hand. Still, each trip posed unexpected and dangerous threats. The more slaves that escaped, the more hunters got into the business of tracking them down. Fugitives did whatever they could to get the bounty hunters off their tracks. They poured

Frederick Douglass was a famous black leader who, like Harriet, had been born a slave. But he had learned to read and write as a child. Escaping when he was about twenty years old by pretending he was a sailor, Frederick became a leading abolitionist and published his own newspaper called the *North Star.* As a "stationmaster" on the Underground Railroad, he became great friends with Harriet.

Frederick Douglass

pepper on the trail or traveled through water so that the bloodhounds lost their scents. Instead of trying to get a running start before their masters noticed their absence, some slaves hid close to home until enough time had passed that their owners assumed they were long gone and stopped looking. *Then* they set out for the North.

In all her journeys, Harriet developed a few tricks of her own. She became a master of disguises, sometimes dressing as an old woman or a man. She also disguised her emotions—refusing to show fear. Once on a mission, when she and her passengers came upon a group of whites while crossing a bridge, Harriet walked right up to them and started a conversation as if it were the most ordinary thing in the world. Her passengers quickly followed her lead, and soon everyone was walking and laughing like they were having the greatest time ever. The whites assumed only free blacks could act so carefree.

Harriet had her fair share of close calls. When

some slave hunters were nearing her group at a train station, she made everyone board a train going south—the opposite direction of the way they wanted to go. But the maneuver worked. Why would escaped slaves get on a train going south? Again, they passed unnoticed.

Another time, back in her hometown, where it was especially easy for her to get caught, Harriet was buying some chickens at the market when she saw her former owner approaching!

Harriet's Tips for a Successful Trip

- Travel in late fall or winter, when the nights are long and the days are short.

- Leave on Saturday night for a head start, because slaves won't be missed on Sunday, their day off.

- Pay free blacks to tear down reward notices as soon as owners tack them up.

- Meet in cemeteries, so that a group of slaves looks like ordinary mourners.

- Don't tell anyone except those who absolutely need to know about your plans.

- Carry a gun.

- No one is allowed to turn back for any reason . . . ever.

She had to think fast. Harriet startled some chickens, which began squawking and flapping so much, that they caught the attention of the owner, who paid no mind to Harriet.

Harriet never strayed from her mission, no matter what, even if she was sick, tired, hungry, or in pain. Her ability to go for days with hardly any sleep or food was legendary. Once she had an infected tooth that was getting

progressively worse along a trip. Getting help was simply too dangerous, so she knocked out her top row of teeth with the handle of the gun she always carried. Now *that's* commitment.

Despite all her successes, Harriet still hadn't helped any members of her immediate family go north. Three of her brothers had tried to escape a few times between 1851 and 1854, but they were always caught. Part of the problem was that they were watched even more closely than ordinary slaves because of Harriet's growing fame. Her reputation for bravery, smarts, and strength became common knowledge among **abolitionists** (people who wanted to end slavery). During the 1850s, Harriet began speaking at antislavery rallies in the North, where people were fascinated with her story and the charming way she told it. (Public appearances, however, were tricky business for a fugitive. They were always a

Harriet guided so many people to freedom that she got the nickname Moses. Just like Moses in the Bible, who led the Jews out of their slavery in Egypt, so she led black people from theirs in the South. "I was the conductor on the Underground Railroad for eight years," Harriet said, "and I can say what most conductors can't say—I never ran my train off the track and I never lost a passenger."

surprise, so that slave hunters couldn't use events to catch her.) In the long black skirt and black hat she always wore, this tiny lady had audiences gripped with her lively, hair-raising, and inspiring tales.

Although it would be especially hard to rescue her family, again circumstances gave Harriet no choice but to try. On Christmas Eve 1854, she arrived back home to collect her brothers Robert, Ben, and Henry, who were going to be sold two days later. They got off to a tough start when Robert's wife went into labor. He just couldn't go until she had the baby. Harriet and her other brothers Ben and Henry had to make the difficult decision as to

whether they should wait for him and risk all their lives, or go ahead without him. They left while Robert stayed until his baby was born, even though his tearful wife insisted he go, too, rather than be sold deeper into the South.

Luckily, Robert was able to catch up with his siblings at their first hiding place, a corncrib near their parents' cabin. Their father knew what was going on and brought food to their hiding place. But not their mother, who would have been too upset about their leaving to keep quiet. So as Harriet and her brothers set out for the long journey, they took one quick, heartbreaking last look at their mother sitting in a rocking chair on Christmas Day, waiting for her sons to show up for Christmas dinner.

On December 29, they arrived in Philadelphia, which was not a destination but a stop. After the Fugitive Slave Act passed in 1850, which stated that runaway slaves had to be returned to their masters even if they were found in a free state, Harriet didn't feel her brothers would be safe until they made it all the way to Canada, where slavery was illegal. "I wouldn't trust Uncle Sam with my people any longer," she said. At the turn of the New Year, she and her brothers settled 11 miles across the border from the United States, in

a town called St. Catharines. They might not have had to worry about slavery, but the cold Canadian winter they faced without warm clothes or heat was just as harsh.

No matter where Harriet lived, it wouldn't be home without her parents. In June 1857, she went back south again. This time, it was for her mom and dad. Ben and Rit were now free, so they should have been able to leave whenever they wanted. But they were suspected of hiding a group of runaway slaves who had been caught, and word was that Ben was going to be arrested. So again it was up to Harriet to save the day. In their seventies, Ben and Rit couldn't walk 100 miles. Harriet knew that, and she brought along a horse and cart to carry them until they were far enough away to take a train.

Ben and Rit were overjoyed to be reunited with their children and with the grandchildren they had never met, but winter in St. Catharines was even harder on them.

A couple of years after they moved way up north, William H. Seward, a senator from

Auburn, New York, who was outspoken about ending slavery, made Harriet an offer she couldn't refuse. He sold her some property surrounded by lovely farms and an apple orchard for $1,200. Even better than the good deal was that Harried only had to put twenty-five dollars down and could make payments that fit her budget. Harriet and her parents were finally home.

By the Numbers

No one was a better and braver conductor than Harriet. Her fearlessness helped her break records.

13 Harriet's trips on the Underground Railroad

70 slaves she brought as passengers to freedom

56 other slaves who used her directions to gain their freedom

0 passengers she lost on the Underground Railroad

CHAPTER FOUR

War Time

Abraham Lincoln, who was against the expansion of slavery in new states joining the country, was elected president in November 1860. Soon after, seven states **seceded** from the Union. South Carolina was the first to decide it wanted to separate from the rest of the United States, followed by Mississippi, Florida, Alabama, Georgia, Louisiana, Texas, and later Virginia, Arkansas, North Carolina, and Tennessee. They called themselves the

Skirts and Pants

Harriet wore a dress during the whole
expedition! When she was helping the slaves
get to the boats, she heard someone shout
an order to run, and after she tripped on her
long skirt, it ripped to shreds until she was
hardly wearing anything at all. If she was ever
going to go on a military raid again, she swore
she'd wear bloomers—the wide, roomy pants
named after Amelia Bloomer, who fought for
women's rights.

Confederate States of America. Slavery was tearing the country apart.

Harriet was ready for war. She hoped the Civil War, which began on April 12, 1861, would mean an end to slavery in the entire country. Certainly, slaves came out in masses when the Union army arrived in the South. They wanted to be free and were ready to join the cause—only the Union troops didn't know how to deal with all these desperate men, women, and children.

The Ultimate War Hero

During the Civil War, Harriet was one busy woman. She didn't just help deal with fugitive slaves, but also spied on the Confederate troops and nursed wounded Union soldiers!

• HARRIET THE SPY

Because she knew how to maneuver without being seen in the swamps, fields, grassy plains, and forests of the South, Harriet made the perfect scout. She was able to sneak into enemy territory and find friends among slaves she met. From them, she learned about the size of the Confederate forces, their location and movements, their **tactics**, and the state of their supplies. This was vital information that she took right back to the Union army.

• HARRIET THE GENERAL

On June 1, 1863, Harriet helped to guide about three hundred black soldiers in the only Civil War battle planned and led by a woman!

In the middle of the night, she and Colonel James Montgomery traveled in the lead boat up the Combahee River in South Carolina to ambush Confederate forces. Harriet's network of spies was essential to their mission by guiding the boat around underwater mines that the Confederate side had placed below the surface of the river. Her spies had also told them about the warehouses filled with food and weapons, which the Union troops then raided or destroyed in their surprise attack, which went off without a hitch. As the boats traveled along the river, black men, women, and children ran from the fields and plantations, desperate to get a ride on the

boat and out of slavery. They carried all their most prized possessions, from pigs to pots full of food to children. The battle was a success in more ways than one. In addition to weakening the Confederate side by diminishing their supplies, they also freed more than 750 slaves! A hundred of them joined the Union army right away.

• HARRIET THE CARETAKER

Harriet met up with a renowned black regiment called the Fifty–fourth Massachusetts. This time she wasn't leading the charge, but rather picking up the rear as a nurse and a cook. She still worked tirelessly, keeping the soldiers fed and alive after they became ill or wounded. Among the 650 men of the regiment were the sons of Frederick Douglass and the grandson of Sojourner Truth—who were Harriet's good friends.

89

Because of Harriet's reputation as a great leader, Governor John Andrew of Massachusetts asked Harriet to help deal with the fugitives. Despite the danger to her life Harriet headed south again. The hardest part wasn't risking her own safety, but leaving her elderly parents, whom she was caring for.

On this trip, Harriet didn't have to stomp through swamps and woods. In May 1862, she traveled on a military ship called the *Atlantic* to South Carolina, where she made a perfect bridge between the slaves and Union soldiers. Because Harriet had grown up a slave, she understood their issues. But she had also spent enough time as a free person to know what they needed to gain their freedom.

Harriet took control of the situation and got everyone organized. On the Union army base, she gave out donations of clothes, medicine, and food. Once there was some order, she made

a washhouse, where she taught the ex-slave women how to work for the Union soldiers by doing useful tasks like cooking, sewing, and washing.

CHAPTER FIVE

Fighting for Everyone's Rights

After the fall of the Confederacy, Harriet returned home to Auburn in October 1865.

She should have been given a hero's welcome; instead she was treated like a second-class citizen on the train ride home. After boarding the train with the half-fare ticket she was told soldiers were entitled to, the conductor said black people couldn't use that kind of ticket. Harriet tried to explain her service, but the conductor was in no mood for

listening. He wanted to get rough. He pulled tiny Harriet by her arm, trying to get her off the train, but she refused. It took at least three men to shove Harriet into the baggage car. Instead of thanks for her service, she got her arm in a sling.

Unpaid Bills

The government never paid Harriet for all her work during the Civil War, so she supported herself by baking pies and making root beer when she wasn't tending to wounded soldiers, helping slaves, or acting as a spy. After the war, she asked the government for back pay for her service, but her petitions were lost.

Harriet was angered by this treatment but far from surprised. She had witnessed racial inequality within the Union army. The black regiments proved they were just as brave as any of the white ones. Still, they weren't paid the same amount. The government paid black soldiers seven dollars a month, while white ones got fifteen. That really bothered Harriet. She wasn't satisfied to see African Americans become free. She also wanted equal treatment.

Harriet needed to ride for half price home to Auburn. She might have been famous, but she definitely wasn't rich. She had just worked for almost four years for free, and her house was filled with people who needed a place to stay. Harriet wouldn't turn away anyone who needed her help.

One of those people was Nelson Davis. A Civil War veteran and a former slave, he found a safe, welcoming place in Harriet's home, and

the two eventually fell in love. Nelson, who was
at least twenty years younger, married Harriet
in a happy church ceremony surrounded by
friends and family on March 18, 1869. Nelson
might have brought Harriet much-needed
companionship, but he had **tuberculosis** and
was often sick, so Harriet was still on her own
when it came to taking care of all the people

who filled up her house. She did everything she could to keep the household afloat, including caring for the apple orchards and tending her own garden. She not only served the fruits and vegetables she grew at her table, but also sold them at fruit stands or by going door-to-door. That wasn't her only job. She also worked as a maid.

Women's Rights

Harriet's belief in equality wasn't limited to race. She also felt that women should have equal rights to men, and that included the right to vote. Black men got the right to vote in 1870, but women of any color were still excluded. Harriet joined the women's suffrage movement—which fought for women's right to vote and hold office—and would often speak at their meetings.

Harriet needed more money than she had, because in addition to taking care of her loved ones, she wanted to continue to support the development of newly freed slaves. Her apples and work as a maid weren't going to cut it. So Harriet did what a lot of famous people do when they need money—she wrote a tell-all memoir.

Harriet didn't know how to read or write, but Sarah Bradford, an abolitionist who had long admired Harriet, wrote down her stories for *Scenes in the Life of Harriet Tubman*. When it came out in December 1868, the book gave Harriet a much-needed paycheck.

When Harriet was almost seventy years old, Nelson died. Because he had fought in the war, she was awarded a widow's pension of eight dollars a month. (She still couldn't get the government to award her the back pay for her own service.) Money continued to be a problem for Harriet. Still, she could always find people who had less than her—and she worked to make their lives better.

For years, she had taken in the poor, sick, and elderly—so much so that not everyone who

sought her help could fit in her small house! Harriet dreamed about creating a home where old people could live out their last days. And when Harriet had a dream, it usually came true. She didn't have much in the way of savings, but she took what there was and bought the 25 acres next to her house for $1,450.

Because she could never raise the money, she turned it over to the African Methodist Episcopal Zion Church in 1903. The Church renamed it the Harriet Tubman Home for Aged and Infirm Negroes and opened the doors in 1908. Three years later, Harriet didn't have the strength to live alone anymore. So she moved into the home she had helped create. Finally, for the first time in her life, others were taking care of her.

On March 10, 1913, Harriet died from pneumonia around the age of ninety-three. Although she had lost the use of her legs and was very weak by the end, she still had the strength of personality and spirit that made her the greatest Underground Railroad conductor of all time. That, however, was only part of her legacy. Harriet, a spy, nurse, and leader during the Civil War, fought with everything she had to end slavery in the United States, before becoming an advocate for women's rights and

an activist for the well-being of the elderly. No matter to whom she was standing up or lending a helping hand, Harriet continued to surprise the rest of the world by far exceeding the expectations of what a small black woman could do. What was her secret? Simply to never give up:

"If you are tired, keep going; if you are scared, keep going; if you are hungry, keep going," she said. "If you want to taste freedom, keep going."

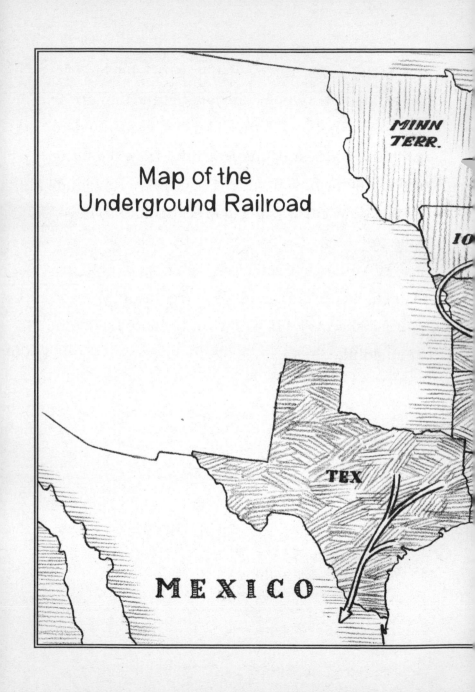

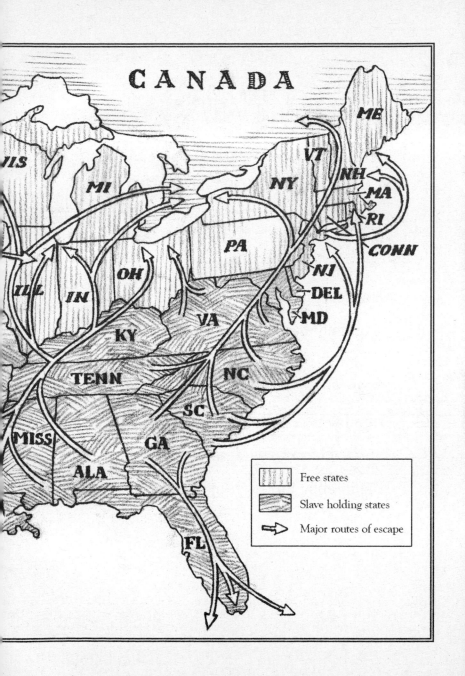

CANADA

Free states

Slave holding states

Major routes of escape

10 Things

You Should Know
About Harriet Tubman

1 Harriet was born a slave, and was originally named Araminta.

2 After an overseer hit Harriet in the head with a heavy weight, she suffered from awful headaches and narcolepsy for the rest of her life.

3 Harriet had one unsuccessful escape attempt with her brothers in 1849, but they made her turn back. She ran away again soon after and made it all the way to Philadelphia.

4 In December 1850, Harriet made her first trip back to the South, to rescue her niece Kessiah.

5 Harriet completed about thirteen trips to the South to free around seventy slaves.

6 On June 1, 1863, Harriet helped command a successful Civil War battle up the Combahee River that resulted in the freeing of about 750 slaves.

7 While she was alive, Harriet was never paid for her four years of service during the Civil War.

8 Harriet became an activist in the women's suffrage movement—which fought for women's right to vote and hold office.

Tubman house

9 Harriet finally settled in Auburn, New York, where she took care of her parents and anyone else who needed help, eventually establishing a home for the elderly.

10 Harriet published a book of her extraordinary adventures told in her words, *Scenes in the Life of Harriet Tubman*, in 1868.

10 MORE Things

That Are Pretty Cool to Know

1 Lots of people wanted to meet Harriet, but she had to be extremely careful that no one was a slave hunter in disguise. So she carried around photos of her friends and made sure anyone who wanted to meet her could identify at least a few of the images.

Silver medal for bravery

2 Although Harriet couldn't read or write, she was friendly with a lot of important intellectuals of her day, such as Ralph Waldo Emerson and Susan B. Anthony.

3 In 1874, Harriet and her second husband adopted a baby girl they called Gertie.

4 In 1897, Queen Victoria bestowed Great Britain's silver medal for bravery on Harriet for her work helping to free slaves.

5 To alleviate the pain of lifelong headaches from her head injury as a kid, she had brain surgery at Massachusetts General Hospital in 1901. Refusing to take medicine to put her to sleep, she bit down on a bullet during the operation in the style of soldiers. She also wanted to walk home—but the doctors insisted she take an ambulance.

6 Harriet was buried with military honors in the Fort Hill Cemetery, right next to her brother.

Statue in
Harlem,
New York

7 President Franklin Delano Roosevelt's wife, Eleanor, christened a ship called the *Harriet Tubman* in 1944.

8 There are monuments dedicated to Harriet all over the world, including in Ghana, New York, and Boston.

A group of students from Albany, New York, on a school trip to stops on the Underground Railroad were shocked to learn Harriet was never compensated by the U.S. government for her service during the Civil War. To right that wrong, they appealed to Hillary Clinton, who was then a senator from New York. The politician got Congress to give $11,750 to the Tubman Home in Auburn, which bought furniture from the period when Harriet lived for visitors to the house.

Tubman
biographies

10 There have been many kids' books written about Harriet's life, but until 2003, there were only two published adult biographies—including Sarah Bradford's book—about this important American heroine!

Glossary

Abolitionist: someone who worked to abolish slavery before the Civil War

Fugitive: someone who is running away, especially from the police

Maneuver: a difficult movement that requires planning and skill

Narcolepsy: a disorder which results in sudden and uncontrollable attacks of sleep

Plantation: a large farm found in warm climates where crops such as coffee, rubber, and cotton are grown

Secede: to formally withdraw from a group or an organization, often to form another organization

Tactics: plans or methods to win a game or battle or achieve a goal

Tuberculosis: a highly contagious disease caused by bacteria that usually affects the lungs

Places to Visit

Harriet had to face danger at every turn on her many trips to free slaves, but your journey in discovering more about her amazing life will be much more enjoyable. Whether online or in real life, check out these places the brave lady visited under much different circumstances.

Bucktown Village Store, Cambridge, Maryland
The store where Harriet refused to help the overseer tie up another slave for a beating and was then hit by the weight that caused her lifelong headaches.
tourdorchester.org/attraction.php?attraction=15

Harriet Tubman Home, Auburn, New York
harriethouse.org

Harriet Tubman Marker, Bucktown, Maryland
hmdb.org/marker.asp?marker=3956

Harriet Tubman Museum and Educational Center, Cambridge, Maryland
harriettubmanorganization.org

Harriet Tubman Underground Railroad Byway
A 125-mile self-guided tour with stops that relate to Harriet's life. The entire route goes from south to north in the same way that slaves traveled.
byways.org/explore/byways/2260

Harriet Tubman Underground Railroad State Park, Dorchester County, Maryland
(Scheduled to open in early 2013.)
dnr.state.md.us/publiclands/eastern/tubman.asp

The Underground Railroad
nps.gov/nr/travel/underground/ugrrhome.htm

Bibliography

Harriet Tubman: A Photographic Story of a Life, Kem Knapp Sawyer, DK Publishing, 2010.

Harriet Tubman: A Woman of Courage, the editors of *Time for Kids* with Renée Skelton, HarperCollins, 2005.

Harriet Tubman: Conductor on the Underground Railroad, Patricia Lantier, Crabtree, 2009.

Harriet Tubman: Leading the Way to Freedom, Laurie Calkhoven, Sterling, 2008.

Who Was Harriet Tubman?, Yona Zeldis McDonough, Grosset & Dunlap, 2002.

Index

Also Available:

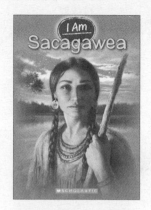

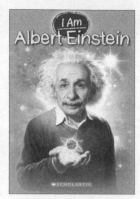